BROKEN KINGDOM

BROKEN KINGDOM

Michelle Bitting

RiskPress

Published by RiskPress
825 Gravenstein Highway North, Suite 12
Sebastopol, California 95472

Published in the United States of America
Copyright © Michelle Bitting, 2018

ISBN: 978-0-9848403-6-6

Cover painting:
Alex Kanevsky
"Hollis"
2015, oil on panel, (detail)
www.dolbychadwickgallery.com

Inside left flap photograph:
Bradley Greer

Inside right flap painting:
Emmet VR Abrams
"Broken Kingdom"

Inside cover photograph:
Alexis Rhone Fancher

Back cover photograph:
Michelle Bitting
"Hollywood & Vine: so glad to meet you, Angeles"

Book design:
Charlie Pendergast and Kevin Connor

Printed in China
by Global PSD

Uncle, what ails thee?
~ Parzival to King Anfortas

Home is where I want to be,
but I guess I'm already there.
~ Talking Heads

Contents

Burnt Offerings

Touched

Jubilate Deo

Escape

An Hour North of Lee Vining, California

Who remembers where we stopped
for jars of orange neon cheese and the tangled black
knots of faux flies my father taught me to thread,
hooks that pierced the lips of bright trout
skimming lagoons in the craggy High Sierra?
I remember ghost lines cast to blue nothingness
we watched dissolve in the lake's dark bottom.
What did we say to each other, side by side,
swaying in the wooden dish? Or was it
just the music of the wind in trees parting
ash-white branches, the Aspen banter?
Why don't I remember reeling with the rush
of my glittering first catch, the zagging colors cinched?
I think it's come to the moment
he showed me how to haul a fat fish up,
how to grasp it tight in my girlish hand,
the wriggling slickness releasing life
into my nervous palm as I raised it high above me
and in one grand swoop, brought the stunned head
down against our boat's iron edge, a gavel felled,
a verdict delivered, stunning those wide round eyes
to stillness. *I can be as cruel as you,*
I wanted to say, with pride, but didn't
and still don't. It's enough
to think of it now. Enough to toss it back,
to let that ugly beauty go.

Home

I reject you in theory,
I become you with practice.

Mostly,
you pulse in memory:
walks to the school

yard, street scent
of anise, dry sage,
the kicked-up ghosts

of sycamore leaves. It was night
and holy carols rang out

against cold December stars.

My hands a white
loaf wrapped in
rabbit fur.

Mary Janes scuffing asphalt
en route to adore the hippie actors

who posed in a storage shed
behind the church parking lot.

Mary and Joseph and the shepherds
crowning a hay-filled manger.

Green floodlight glow,
a bored donkey chewing straw.

Threads of gold shooting from its mouth.

The babe in Mary's arms
swaddled so tight inside blue cloth
we couldn't see his face

but we believed the scene real enough
to suspend.

If only to see before the fact:
unbandage the weeping pus,
the shattering awe

about to descend.
An unexpected masterpiece

or the grown man found in time
with a belt around his neck.

The hideous and beautiful
peered into beforehand.

What keeps taking our breath away.

Even Jesus knew
what was coming
and tried to strike a deal,

crying out.

I'm tired. Of piercings,
the streams of terrified eyes

facing down
the barrel of a gun.

Frankincense and myrrh
can't mask the smell,

keeping it pretty
this time of year

like we did back then,
cloaked in red
and velvet pinafores.

Topiaries for our teachers
made from acorns and pods,

we'd fill our pockets
walking winter streets.

Fathers on the couch
nodding off with drink.

Where were the Wise Men?

Violins, our earnest recitals
after roast beef and Yorkshire,
the eve of our savior's birth.

Good times, I guess, at a distance.
I'm trying to make my own now.

Most nights I get as far as the candle.

Pompeii

Because the worst catastrophes
always come without warning.
Because I never knew who was already
several buckets of rust to the wind
in other chambers. On the blue floor
of my bedroom,
turning the key to my roller skate a few
notches tighter, it could come.
Or dragging the tines of a hairbrush
through my unruly ends, watching
a kingfisher dance
along the slats of the backyard fence,
black crown flashing in the sun. The rumblings
would startle a far-off room,
tremors snaking floorboards until I felt it:
shock waves seeping through doors,
finding my lower holes and gut,
my throat suddenly sucked of all its decent moisture,
voice morphing to pumice as I froze,
roar of the rupture between others
obliterating time and sense
of who I was.
When I return years later,
inspect the pockets preserved by ash
and lack of air beneath heavy layers
like a tongue depressor keeps a sick girl mum
until she coughs it out, the treasure's no
longer silent.
Thirty-one silver coins, four finger rings
and a candelabrum sing. Spaces
where bodies fell, clean and
intact if I try.
I prod them with my sharpened point
so the pictures resume: contorted bodies,
mouths and fists spinning like chariots,
vases and drapes clutched in desperation,
a flowery blur of flames.
My mother's face melting
as her men, her mountaintops,
keep erupting and won't stop
until we're all ghost
monuments, cast in the act of
fleeing our unnatural disaster,
our mesmerizing human fire.

Drought

People of this city
mourning the death of your sacrificial lawns
tendered brown and bald by absent moisture,
behold: the Emerald City returns
after one brief, bold rain. It's lush
and free, go roll around in it, God's
green money, his truly begotten girl.
Call it what it is—Walt's ambrosia,
Lorca's dog food—and we will get
down on all fours and eat it for eternity
after we've fried it with our pallid thumbs,
our flapping tongues without gloves
entering the house of horticultural prayer.
It is a Sunday in winter
and everywhere people are rising
to the sound of the sky's applause.
They're dressing for worship,
slipping on brushed-cotton oxfords,
shined-up loafers, dabbing
or slapping their cheeks with lemon aftershave
and salmon rouge, weaving ribbons through
braided locks still damp from the tub.
Ablutions before oblations. Have you ever stopped
to consider all that water in the Bible?
John splashing himself silly, Jesus's feet,
the perilous storms, and parting a red pond
that longs to separate from its maker? While clouds
above me hammered nails against wooden slats last night,
I thought of it, watching dark fluid
pool on linoleum beneath Billy's head,
the suicide man-child in *One Flew Over the Cuckoo's Nest*,
and how the colossal, dark-haired Chief
hoists that marble column at the end,
extracts it like a root, like a Titan's tooth,
a pillar, a tree trunk, unmooring the monolith font
from the bathroom floor while the camera zooms in
and water floods out
like a pulpit bleeding. And when he hoists
that terrible weight onto his mute, Herculean shoulder
like a cold white cross, and heaves it through
the window, smashing the past, the dagger droplets
of glass, that's like water too, that scattering
of shards, a final cleansing and the last image
of Chief no one will ever forget: his big body
lumbering free into the distant mist,
dissolving against gray fields, the giant paddles
of his feet kicking up behind, a slow-motion wheel
rolling over grass that is like green water
and he can walk on it.

On O'Hara's Birthday

The sun behind the hills
is *a big bald head*
as Laurie Anderson once put it

and the wind so fierce last night
it whipped the feeder
from its wire

so the squirrels got to gorge
on thistle seed all morning
leaping Errol Flynn–style

from branch to ledge to Adirondack seat
whatever gullible shapes
that got in their way, smashed

mirroring my rage
stuck here in the trough
of stormy times

where the president says
grab all you can!
the book of decency

an illusion, see
he has no clothes
strolls a midtown avenue

waving his shaft in God's face
the tunnels of our ears
internment camps

our bodies passed out
on the collective human cot
wings pass over

an extermination
of the soul
yes, I said the soul

I know it's indulgent
like cupcakes
but I like cupcakes

on anyone's birthday!
real buttercream frosting
and authentic wild vanilla

the risen batter ribboned
with flecks of shaved bean
like little black bells

ringing the steeples
of your taste buds
calling you back home

wherever that is
in case you can't remember
the place of sweetness

oh, Lord
let us please
feel innocent again

Autumn Deluge

The amber tree
of coral leaves
its contagion spreading
Rough sidewalks
and running past
I snap a picture
with my portable eye
the light-bearing
cell I wobble without
Thinking Rothko
seeing everything's
a cross a crucifixion of sorts
lines and colors
singing out
against wet grass
Waking up this way
my mind wants to burst
its dark-dreaming suit
the thin cartoon
and algae spool
A river can rise
out of nowhere
sweep everything off
And you won't rule
water only invent
new ways of swimming
your raft
a ragged ledge
made of brooms
a certain face
the familiar blunt mustache
resurfacing tries
to insert itself
History
in tangled clumps
a daisy chain
of shade tossed
to the stifled pond where
the latest monster
the flip dictator
who faked it
to get elected
waves from the edge
pretending to be kind
pretending he's here
to save you

Broken Kingdom

What does it take
for winnowed brain cells

and ligaments, layers
of skin tissue stretched

thin as phyllo dough,
to sound the alarm?

To know we are
but flashing mementos,

flesh remnants
of ever-crumbling rooms?

Let us tear the curtains down,
let our real suns in. What is

your soul's net worth, anyway?
The Egyptians understood.

A feather of gold weighed
when you're no longer there.

You make a choice,
stake your consequences

and in the final moment
risk remorse: the forgone kisses,

a child's touch,
the way her hair smells

of ocean and brine. The grit,
a pink throne of oiled scalp

and tangled clouds,
beach of abandoned shells

your face shovels deep into now,
this broken kingdom

where all you want anymore
is to lay yourself down

and be buried alive.

Bricolage

But what in fact will we make from it this time?
The double-gutted panes,
twin stamps
of broken glass, a jagged abyss
in the glittering desert
he pointed his knobby index through—
scopes and barrels,
the decision to aim, press
as if taking a pulse,
filling his finger,
the dead space inside
with all he could shatter.
And still something converged,
wanting to build
in the chaos, the complete absence.
Heroes in the dark
answering a call,
not knowing until now
their names were written
on smoke and bone. They
covered the fallen,
making a shield,
taking metal in the back.
Some were just born that way,
to take what the moment gives
and make a bridge
or song of it—
refrains of sky
ripped open, a carnage of stars
to look up to
in the terrible after. How
one stopped to bend
over another, like a halo
or breast—the mother in everyone
stepping from shadows
to feed the forsaken world.
Tableaus of radiance
no museum will ever tire
of unfurling for display.
How many masterpieces though,
how many times
must we kneel, dumbstruck
before the miracle,
before we say *Enough*—
I remember what matters.
Please don't ever remind me again.

What the Rain Made

Water fallen from skies
scraped of clouds & moisture
now bloats the heads of succulents.
Siphoned juice seeps through soil
and the once-desperate flora suddenly float:
green stubs like chubby babies' fingers,
watered organs that want to burst: balloons
taking aim on a hot summer day.
Water stemmed from wells
hidden beneath the surface.
Pictures we imagine in the dark with our eyes shut tight.
Seeds tossed, the soil of dreams
brings white-ashed ghosts
who rattle their chains down narrowing halls.
The soup grows thin & salty with reduction.
Centuries fly by and still the same miserable portraits:
bankers & demagogues
turning red in the face like monkeys
show delight through their behinds.
I thought we were done with this.
But we are never done with this.
Pictures imagined in the dark with our eyes shut tight.
The giant we woke to discover
atop the beanstalk watered daily.
Burro's tail, black prince, snake plants,
aloe. Careful what you wish for.
Stems & roots, the caudices adapt,
storing energy in leaves.
This one's head a red explosion,
a Hindenburg in flames,
flashing through airwaves around us.
What the loam carries: shadows running
to catch the bus as the perfect storm hits.
In the dream, my feet spin pedals and take me nowhere.
Worms come crawling from below
to scribble their dankest hate
across walls of the local high school.
Water in the underworld,
the dead make us yearn for mommy,
who walked into the sea two books ago.
Maybe better to die a hero
than wander an eternity
in this horror show.
Unless you're a mommy.

What the rain brought up: pictures
put to rest fifty years past, zombied to life.
Bodies in trees, hung like ornaments,
our children's mouths
shocked open, struck midsong,
their hallelujahs trying to fly
to a God who does not hear.

November

She imagined the post-election president
with his honorable first lady
cast out and shivering at sea
after the crazy man was chosen,
their bed a perilous boat
they'd toss and turn all night in,
riled by the rabble noise
of two marching bands
clashing in the distance,
songs of people
wailing at the polls, torn
and soiled flags crammed inside
the closing doors
of their ears. Here, the sky booms
with sound, cannon fire
loosed to counter anarchists,
always the last to leave the protest,
having shed their allegiance
to known narrative structures
and the time-space continuum.
I walk with shifting winds
and keep my gaze fixed
on yellow shapes underfoot,
leaves of ginkgo pressed
like preschool hands
into the dark gutters
of wet sidewalks.
I will never feel the same again.
My nerves and lids flicker
when a rush of strangers
marches past. I try
to shift gears, find
the necessary heft required
to bear this future on. The moon

is a mirror I look up into
without flinching, facing
bodies and constitutions,
the dead limbs
that history's buried there. I want a heart
where color vibrates
a million times more vehemently,
I want to dance in its hot,
human glow,
watch its coming eclipse
of the scorching sites
where terrible fires still rage on,
the unseeing centers and edges
of the white, white whites of our eyes.

After

After the kingdom falls
we return to a plain sense of things.
Leaves cling to the dense air,
the old man bound to a hospital bed
sucks his morphine sap
and nods off
to lands I'll never recognize. A
cup of coffee is what it is as I
write this. Grateful.
For this dark fluid sun,
a few trails of cream
funneled into
my green alembic belly,
scouring my inner forest
of its antique tint
to make room for the coming sugar.
Pale powder, cold to the tongue,
we make brave angels in.
Trees that have no time
or heart left
and in cahoots with boastful winds
shake a sick filament down.
Though it shimmers
as fool's gold will,
it can fuck off
in the absence of real imagination.
I pay attention
to burgeoning vines

fingering the cracks
of ruddy timbers. Their presence
an unmistakable contrast,
the old steroid-stuffed trunks
silently squeezed
by such delicate ink,
an intricate tattooing, new DNA
in fiery-red flourish
that becomes the breath of life.
The great structure will morph
into a minor house
where there is room for everyone
as I see it. Who thinks of twine?
Of training bodies to a lattice, your tainted
holy light? Once I thought
I could wander lush arbors,
the lurid shade
of your selective gardens,
and feel our mutual wombing.
But, *Maestra,*
your *greenhouse never so badly needed paint,*
your fence a hundred years old
and rotting at the base,
your gates and screws
of exclusion coming loose. Thank God
for the dog
that didn't sniff the infested opening
and run off
already,
didn't escape this
yard's
dissolving,
unhinged void,
as we all will
someday soon
when you're not
looking
and the end
becomes the beginning.

BURNT OFFERINGS

It is gentleness and torture. It is cookery and it is apocalypse.
~ Gaston Bachelard, *from* The Psychoanalysis of Fire

Twenty Years Later in a Kitchen

We are things of dry hours and the involuntary plan. We
wind the clocks and forget why we are,
set our minds and hands to daily buzzing things:
scraping toast, the gimp dog's bandages, a coupon citadel and wisps of
emerald cuttings so long in the sun their funereal pots go dry.
Where is the gold we foraged, sweet milk of the subterranean hours?
Once I spoke in ritual tongue: our lips touched, a skirt twirled, and
my eyes said: *Take flight on wings of smoke and flame.* The
chariot burning, blood and sky between bodies rose, lit with an involuntary
moan. Now memory opens, a mighty aphrodisiac unleashed. This was the plan.

Recipe for Disaster

But the child being born malicious stirs up the mania for storytelling.
    ~ Gaston Bachelard, from The Poetics of Reverie

I learned to cook by trial and error
the same as I learned to live
running through the house
with scissors in my hand
opening books
to strange and random pages
a natural-born pyro
I turned on the stove
my flimsy nightie poofed
to fly up in flames
a taste that's hard to categorize
pumpkin pie and coriander
cumin ground to specks
à la mode of destruction
and since I never learned
to clean up right
when I lost the sealing caps
all the aromas flew out
like bags of godly winds
my sailor pages flared
loose as you'd expect
a pension for flavors
foraged at night
and just enough unhinged
to suit a heretic's tongue: Chaos
your parasol spinning
over my left shoulder
like a Black Sun
when day refuses to lift
its lead curtain
one's wings fly nowhere but down
to dirt and ash
I was born with the right ingredients
flecks in my father's eyes
the bitter, broken grains
floating up from dreams
sunken fleets of the girls I am
gathering in memory
I can almost see them now
hailing me from the crags
their outstretched hands

moon-glow pearls
kept in my crippled pocket
because my fingers laced
become a steeple shape—song
and every voice turned inside out
crowned in unison
then dashed against rocks
undoing flesh and bone
the pleasure of seeing blood
of tracking red threads
serpents in The Garden
that lead to The Book
before The Beginning: womb,
crevice & the warmest placenta halos
everything longed for
in a buried stream
in underworlds of hope
where heroes are naturally born
and how could I not eat that up?

Little Red Car

The Father's heart is a little red car
he parks in the garage with his golf clubs and gun.

The Father's heart is his father's heart in a wheelchair
with a black hat on.

The Father's heart is a truckload of tomatoes,
a dead Vargas girl tucked
under its mounds of waxy fruit.

The Father's heart bleeds and bleeds into a glass tumbler.
He drinks it over ice every day at half past five.

When The Father dozes off, the moon creeps up
the walls of his big house, its oleander eye

making the trees flicker outside.
And the leaves

on the ghost trees quiver. He wakes and looking out
sees his children in their green, glowing shapes.

The Father's heart leaps with longing; it reels,
but the windows are shut, sealed tight.

And nothing, not even his God, gets in.

Back Then I Wanted to Paint like Rauschenberg

And so fingering the pleats on my uniform skirt, I scoured the walls of the high school darkroom for signs of intelligence. I found them developing in trays of dangerous chemicals under the glare of a red safety bulb. Also in the cloth of many colors flowing from my art teacher's mouth. Some of this I snipped and collaged into a self-portrait that may also have contained rags from my mother's costumes: red sequins with fringe around the hips worn to raise money for the Junior Leagues of America. Also the fork my father stabbed repeatedly into my brother's meatloaf whenever he looked away, as he often did, to stare out the window at whatever the void was making, grateful for the golden flight of bees, the Euclidean patterns their bodies made swarming in and out of honeycomb chambers cached in a weeping pepper tree. Such sweet hell to navigate! All those sticky rings of hidden infernos, the puzzling innards. In the spirit of Rauschenberg, who glued whole chickens and refrigerators, barbed wire, tin cans, rope, astronauts, sprung sofa recliners, doorknobs, you name it, into his paintings, my self-portrait contains anything I care to pin to it, such as various album covers of LPs my brother spun for me over and over on Saturday mornings: Tom Verlaine, the Band, and Joni Mitchell's *Miles of Aisles* were pretty crucial. I can see us now, lounging in our pajamas, the smell of stinky socks and strawberry pancakes vying for alpha prominence in the dog park of our nostrils. The painting of my life would not be complete without a snapshot of the last time I saw my brother Will, only I don't own that. If I'd known he wasn't coming back, I would have paid more attention. Nor do I know anymore what happened to the picture of him I carried around in my brown fringe hippie purse for so long before handing it to a sympathetic cop in the lobby of that grand and scary Yosemite hotel the time my brother went off his meds and drained the minibar in his room. He wandered into a sunset of giant sequoias and fiery orange-red skies with nothing but the clothes on his back and a whack compass spinning like a circus clown inside his head. The sky a big blank canvas he walks into and disappears.

Burnt Offerings

No older than ten and sucking Fresca
from blue aluminum in a wooded LA canyon,
I wandered the quiet street alone, past
the mysterious burnt-down house.
Back and forth I crossed it,
fascinated by the scarred frame,
the pitch-incinerated beams
and tattered doorways
like old ladies in soiled negligees,
scorched bricks and remains of a fireplace
that felt ironic under the circumstances.
Nearby, a tree grew, bloated and gnarled,
billowed with umber fungus.
And this sidewalk grotesquery,
the blight consuming trunk and root base,
fed my obsession, the way the saucer-hewn sponges
that infiltrated bark armor,
splitting open the oak's rough living skin,
matched the peculiar handiwork
of whatever made fire touch down in the first place,
eating up walls and lintels,
lace curtains, shoe racks, and teddy bears,
the still-smoking inferno that reeked of damp,
acrid charcoal and sickly sweet ruins
crazy nature had left behind. Accidents will happen,
although hardly without invitation,
the material world craving it, the soul leaping blood-first
to its purging. To denude, to undress,
to wear a lampshade for a crown
and become flame dancing on altars
reflecting wine's redness reaching aloft
to mingle music with the spheres. Things you know
but can't say, urped. The unburied life.
This is what I sensed but only silently.
Silt that builds up, daring forces to bear down, naturally.
Like ships locked in require ghosts
and significant dredging to exit the bay, bucket by bucket.
So beautiful to behold their unharnessing then.
Muck sailed through on a map scaled to freedom,
this heaven where I knew I might someday find myself.

She Was a Dark-Hearted Child

Just like Rumpelstiltskin
and she was shaping a mask.

One side, her father.
The other, her mother.

She fit herself
inside the pasty interior,

this bunker of a home:
her own private foxhole.

She loved them
for their finer points.
There were many

and besides, the mask was seared
to skin, defying science

and any earnest
attempts to dissolve
their alien arrangement.

This mess,
her own making
that made her.

Death flaunted
their relationship, throttling
the doldrums

that make an ordinary day flow.

While she
sat tapping
keys,
a code to liberation.

The war was long and cold.
Everything morphing,
becoming bone.

Transformation, that spent term
promising too-easy relief.

She grasped it anyway,
her killing strokes,
and tried to love them as they were.

Where does loathing leave one
except alone in a bathroom,

scalpel poised
to chart the mirror image?

No one knows what it's like,
Skin-close inside
the cave, ripe traces of DNA

festering along trails
of snot and eyelash glue.

Now she conversed with stars
and tapped the solitary
walls of confinement.

Her legs in flames
from all the leaping.

Mother, what a great cook you are,
she said.

How splendid your cheekbones
and desire to please,
your beloved causes.

She said, needing to love her
before they've flown.

But was there any room left
in that whirlpool
of white flowers

and church pews? Everything
assessed
relative to that?

Her father's heart was failing.
Case closed. The owner of them
all.

She thought: The day my child
casts my likeness
to the ground and stomps,

please light a candle
and celebrate.

I swear to God,
say what you want.

No more need,
no dark secret burning
—holes

to hear my own name.

Come now, she said.
We know an act of love when we see it.

December 20, 2016

I learned a lot from the free museum lecture on the Reformation,
how it wasn't really Holy or Roman or an Empire at all
when I step back and let the big picture blur. That night
at the trattoria, a stranger with thinning gray wisps
and shadow for shave declared himself sober thirty years
for all the restaurant to hear. He spat mouthfuls of red liquid
into an urn, blood-colored murk from goblets that were lined up
like spent soldiers around his manic face at the tasting table.
I could feel the unspoken wars, swirling and tense in his
high-priced tannins. That night, he gave me a bad painting he'd made.
My patience for unbidden gifts with conditions grows weary
with age: little indulgences, hidden fund-raisers,
the politicians buying their way to the top, heaven a gilded
locker room under the moon's yellow eye, glowing wide.
Even Martin Luther had a change of heart for the darker
when he began to lack followers. In the beginning,
God fed the rules to the horizon, his dogs crying in constellation,
and I've been staring up at the sky, amazed, ever since,
like I do at the fine-cut stars flashing me from pawnshop windows
I pass, stumbling toward home on the darkest day of the year.

Portrait of Cafe with Young Schizophrenic Couple

They enter, and the customers in line step back,
a human chain yielding to the heat

of walking insanity. As if for royalty. As if for
senators. Or chain-saw-carrying

maniacs. For Jesus and Mary in T-shirts,
their stringy, unwashed hair and sweaty pits

doomed to wander the waking day,
freak shows flashing on endless loop

across their minds' funhouse screens.
There ought to be a law. They ought to get

a medal. I think they are in love. Milk froths
in the baristas' hands, machines blasting mist

as blades grind another pound of Ecuadorian
roast to a fine, drinkable dust. Flocks of ghost

birds flush up to a crack in the ceiling
and the girl's gaze follows them, her head

cocked and trailing to a spot where the bulbous
fixture has come unslung from its stucco roost.

For her thin-grimaced regard, this might be like
watching a cow give birth to a calf

in clown face. Or like my brother once imagined, Nazis
listening through the chimney from a dark, starless sky.

Your worst dreams come alive. Her boyfriend totally
understands. They giggle together at telepathic cartoons,

connected by current, the twisted rope taut between.
See how his eyes pulse, his mouth twitches in response

to her moment's mental distress? So he leans in closer,
taking her nightmare in as the normal world

bustles around its busy way. While the beasts
of delusion sing on, their imaginary teeth

gnashing the flesh of young lovers to pieces.
And in places we can't see, they bleed.

27

There's Nothing Wrong

in that tender way
you merged
with the dying world
without terror
or torment cloying
Cutting your clumsy
hand on fumbled crystal
Bleeding out
at the unexpected news
No latching on
Your quivering infant lips
clamped to the breast
of *say it ain't so*
A baby wailing at dusk
for her mother
You'd left that ghost
in her white-aproned house
long ago
Nothing back then
but you
and the hollow shadow
of the cross
its ailing males
trumpets raised
above the family cornucopia
Like a dove
you surrendered
to spoon-feed
Folded your rose
into your mother's
and her mother's warm immigrant kitchen
Cabbage rolls and paprikash
we women learned
to shape
Never running
fast or far enough
to keep from testing
that eerily sweet trickle
The roughest lessons
lost brothers
taken in stride
And it's enough
There's comfort to be found
Because you walked so far

through catastrophe
bonfires of hypocrisy
unswept ruins
of shattered grace
and mazy light
Love nonetheless felt
if fractal
through blades of glass
Learning how
it really is true
To live and wake each moment
in a war-won scrap
of sun
Your cheek turned to it
pressed to the pink
sleeves of tulips
simply that once more
made it through winter
You are here to proclaim
their reckless beauty
in spite of the cold hard earth
broken through
And into whose quiet bed
they will without
a seed of doubt
like you
someday return

Glimmers and Limbo (Fugue State #1)

The paths not yet walked, impossible green, verdure sewn to the falls

and mists of memory entered there: *water in light, limbo being aquatic.* Oh Bridal Veil, oh curtains pleated with iron and rain, rapturing, pine-scented, weaving your wet gold threads through streams of wandering skin. *In my dream I just get up and fly, feeling prayed over.*

Kissed by absence, chance meetings, the way it was

so good to leave one city and travel south, this *life in the slowness of limbo, a certain layer of births,* entering that town of tattooed sailors when darkness arrived. *Childhood is a human water, a water which comes out of the shadows,* and feeling thirsty

I stepped into the hotel hallway late to find two girls wielding sequins, glue guns, a bag of pointy, velvet leaves. On their knees, festival costumes stretched along the carpet's labyrinth, they turned to me, surprised: "This one's a mermaid, this one is poison ivy," they each said, smiling, their faces twin suns shining down a night corridor.

What a lot of beings we have begun! Faint scent of marijuana on their breath. I choked up, seeing them. *What a lot of lost springs which have, nevertheless, flowed!*

Young beauties, your eyes demurring, your slender hands an industry buzzing above needles and cloth, shaping starlight from scrap. *In reverie we reenter into contact, possibilities.*

In search of ice, I loved the world again.

The Slaying

And all this writing on the wall / Oh I can read between the lines.
   ~ Dire Straits, from "Hand in Hand"

The old art room
alone there with light
from the canyon
spilling in through Spanish windows
I was thinking about
your hands at work
touching color to canvas
I wanted them
to touch me
while I busied myself
in the dark
jiggling images in trays
my vinegar cave
palms wet
the crimson glow
of miniature mouths
and eyes
floating up through chemicals
my world
coming into focus
This was the beginning
where commandments were written
on hours made of water
explosions
in my private parts
colorful displays
like fireworks in fountains
no one but us
could see
When I finally came of age
and ran
the mountain down
every inch
of me liquefied
I wandered
another hundred years
through dry deserts
graffitied by
circling vultures
This was a long time ago
Emily Dickinson
understands

She hands over
her tidy white bloomers
and I wrap
my best appendages
notes from
the back of my throat
ready to unreel
the imaginary
I'm coming home
with my sins intact
having cleared
the giant wailing
crags of
mandibles oceans
of disruption
I've buried
myself on this
shore deep in ash
barely a flame kept alive
The sea no longer terrifies
but erases
the suitors' gaze
overgrown like cancer
lines woven in sand
a scaffolding of wombs
I unravel the loom
and begin the story again

TOUCHED

And then she poured all her blood into these syllables,
and she offered it to her to drink like this: "You have it."
~ *Hélène Cixous, from* The Book of Promethea

Artisanal Baptismal

At dawn the sea fell back to an acceptable
level, the water forming a wall around us,
the dead on the shore lined up, swaying to the right,
tambourines and dancing to the left. We knew
we'd be needing more of it, before the last
heavy bird had his way, beak to carrion,
the running fish, silent, shocked, and silvery.
The choir was there, in the darkness, a flame
to lean into. The singers in stitched red cassocks,
the pit and giant organ, a minotaur behind us.
We were sweating our songs out, little balls
of wetness trembling inside our blouses. I sang
to the upright human candles, pillars of
fire and smoke, and pledged to stand solid
atop crumbling vestiges, dividing parties,
gods & waves overwhelming the congregants
(how fast they could run in sandals back then!),
clutching our newborn baby heads, pigskin balls
passed over. We sprinted for the line, birthed ourselves
through collapsing superstructures, lips shuddering
apart, and felt the spirit move, our tears mixed
with prayed-over waters. If the dunking and kiss
of clove-laced oil made us cry, caressing our bony
crowns, know it only meant we were born with the Devil
already in us, pathogens we'd grown our own immunity to,
a community garden: worms, pestilence, the sin of leaves
decaying, acidic stenches, rotting citrus, besotted compost,
a suicide we embraced, strapped to our chests, dive-bombing
the loam a thousand leagues down, where the group hug
ignited, sparking green, so the parachute could open—rainbow
wounds in trepid bloom—shape of a flower and offered
by hand to the most delicate, endangered you.

Stripped, Genesis

It's raining and a man runs down the road
in nothing but red shorts and T-shirt.

Yes, a man might strip himself
of the need to be anything

but a slave to open spaces and belief
that the sun will be his friend

no matter what. I understand the urge
to shed it all: decorum, rules,

rationale. Sometimes I want to cry,
let the floods swarm and dissolve,

morph me into other elements:
a spread of yellow stars

like pixelated butter along wet sidewalk
when maple trees shudder,

giving up their winter ghost.
To wake to my husband

telling me he wept
in his dream last night,

watching a boy starve,
fed only communion wafers.

Nothing more. One might wonder
about Noah being fed

the news of what was to come
that moment on the mountain.

After six hundred birthdays,
one might wonder:

What the fuck, Lord?

watching The Maker
trash his art like that,

the giant painting in the desert
Noah trekked since

he was old enough to herd goats
wiped in one almighty stroke.

Giant vats of gesso poured over,
a so-called restoration.

I'm not averse
to complete erasure:

the heavens drained,
my vision renewed.

There's room for everything.

Especially the arks we build
from grief, paper, from words,

my daughter's smile
pinning her cheek

to my shoulder tonight
as we make a fire

of our own design, light
candles of burnt sugar,

and bow down
to inked imaginings,

smoke curling,
a sweet canoe we step

into and sail away
and no one to say when.

Holy Fool

She lived like an outcast
She lived in the kitchen
Lessons from the farmer's mouth
Coughed hard into saved soup
Red crumbs bled by nuns
Making flames that gathered
inside her mind's expanding eye
She wore rags on her head
and sang in her sleep
The woman afflicted by demons

Touched

You've got that half crown
of raw silk daisies
with the sun-poked centers
wrapped around your head again,
sparks and ribbons streaming
the lashes of winged creatures
sketched into a blue journal
you always carry. I don't know how
we got so lucky
to say we know you well when
clearly you are from somewhere else,
wherever extraterrestrials blossom,
dotting forests
like the white-rabbit pages you inhabit,
like magic mushrooms, every surface
your dark pen sprouts its ink.
But I'm convinced that,
aside from enough chicken nuggets and fries
(which is pretty much all you ate
the first twelve years of your life),
enough soft garments, a sturdy
roof, and fat blankets
to shield the night's cruelest breeze,
the greatest gift
a being may be born with
is to arrive a little touched, antennae
like tiny organic blades
stationed inside the ears and eyes
and hands, which, I suppose
implies a kind of fierce fragility,
a loony willingness
to be opened and receive,
to allow the earth's cosmic squirming
to current your knuckle bones
and throat, calling back
to that strange, unearthly divide.
What the great St. Vincent Millay meant
in one of her finer, broken moments
when she said: *God, I can push the grass apart
and lay my finger on Thy heart.*

sometimes i want to look away

sometimes i want to look away but i never look away. to say we measure progress according to the weather doesn't come close to expressing my newfound passion for plumbing or how tonight i watched the backs of my son and husband bent over a stopped-up bathroom sink, side by side, ungunking the suspect pipes plugged with mucous, hair, and the gooey red tooth gel both teens use. i know you don't get it, the significance. two grown males toiling in tandem and the boy's solemn calm as his father unscrews an elbow joint and they peer down into a cruddy abyss, black with festered fluid and artificial flavors, the rose-scented lotions my girl slathers on her arms. this is where it goes, how we all end up: corroded fluids and epidermis, protein curlicues, cuticles, and eyelash flakes so lovely and aromatic once, like the way a baby smells of yeast and rosemary fresh from the oven, the center moist, the edges golden, the surface buttered with cream and salt. the way it's supposed to be in the beginning but was not with this boy, now a man holding a wrench and an appetite to learn, a patience for mechanical mishaps hard-won over time after eons of volcanic fits. i couldn't bear it almost and we barely survived. you would not have wanted to be there, would have asked to avert your eyes, but i could not. little luxury until now, eighteen years after: father and son clearing the pipes. the labor, the baby, and a decades-long birth, i'm telling you, shit never smelled so sweet.

A Foreboding Urn

~ for the students of Marjory Stoneman Douglas High School

How not to grieve for the generations surging
after us? How not pursue cold truths, the mad impious
gods and wastelands they were fostering,
their marble tongues and desolation
rhymes, reedy refrains piped into the earth
that would haunt the citadels of time, sorrow burning
bare shapes of trees into our once-green Arcady?
A sylvan child stood, leaf-quiet in the forest, beauty
and one hand resting on the silken flank of a lone
heifer lowing our tale of parched seas and coming sacrifice
across the altar of the sky. A flowery garland fringed both,
soul-river breathing her silent melody like a slow kiss,
a long branch extended for their spirited escape. Weary but unfading,
warm bliss, the eternal songs, remained their spring in the making.

City of Angels

The LA River is a memory,
its gulches pinned
with carcasses of cats
tossed to ditch trickle and flies. Museums

bulge here, bright
with taxidermied wonders.
It's like

I've died and float in heaven.

Witness the
apparition: birds
fly overhead,

winged workers
without papers
shitting Pollocks across my windshield.

Let it go, boys. Let it go!

And enter another off-ramp,
another sea
of orange vests and cones,

another road
in perpetual state
of renewal. This life.

If love rains down
will we still love us? The raids

are underway
oversees, launched full swing
and strung from headlines.

So-called enemies
a cell text away

and all this time
I thought we were friends.

One hand clicks
while the other lifts a spoon
of fragrant rice
in a suburban kitchen.

You've never heard silence
that peculiar or loud
falling on
flesh and steel.

There's so much work
to be done.

Now children run
from bricks and mortar
and we can't fill our pages fast enough.

City of speed,
freeway taco stands,
Chinatown,
and Hop Louies

where Singapore slings
still flow,

thanks be to mud.

Of good vibes
and rad wave sets
along a rippled Malibu shore,

matched to the sun gods' abs
and foreheads
of homeless

who fish the innards
of recycling bins
like self-appointed surgeons.

Everyday shit. *Idiot love*
will spark the fusion
from where I sit.

Palm trees nodding off,
bent at the waist
over another traffic stalemate,

the blind burn
of chrome when you
think of it.

All those hearts
and nobody moves.

When the Work Runs Out Again

I try not to be obvious
rationing the waffles.
I worry my beads
through long hours,
marked by the swish
of a cat's voodoo tail,
the empress black and white,
licking herself clean
in time to the click
of the clock's kitchen wand.
I watch the maple tree's fury
ignite the walk outside,
a sudden fire
I know to let rush in,
the magic red flush
that will fuel the furnace later,
when terror creeps
and threatens to freeze me.
Mercy is a mouth,
its cloud of moist heat
exhaled into crisp palms,
prayer relaxing the mind's blue knot,
a tundra place
that melts, clearing a space
in the center of the chest. Whether
or not you agree
with the great poet from Ghana
who claims we've shot our wad
personifying the heart, still,
I trot those game girls out:
mind, body, yes, heart, yes, soul.
There's no dividing the divine
and what remains
takes possession—writhes
and spits
on a wrist of crossed wires:
the pulse point,
a medicine bag descending
from heavenly rafters.
Where the skin of the floor
is met with a cuneiform stone,
the earth and axis mundi,
hot charms of engagement
that get the engines revved.
Where the drums beat so loud
your ears bleed
and then you remember who you are.

Fugue State #2

On the streets of Istanbul
I got lost,

as alien and as at home
as humanly possible.

Minarets sang out
the wailing call to prayer,
a clockwork to race my pulse by.

Blue ships of plenty
docked Aegean adjacent,

barnacle chests bulging nets
of silver mackerel
as I walked past.

Then tea from an hourglass
at the shop Şah Sultan,
color of crushed pomegranate

and served on mirrored trays
by men I couldn't understand.

Turkish delight made of roses
and emerald pistachios,

the white pelt of powdered
sugar melting as I chewed,

an aftertaste that followed me
through Mehmed's mosque
and the Spice Bazaar.

I wanted to roll like a dog in cardamom.

For sapphire pendants
rimmed in crystal ice
to wink evil at me everywhere.

Eyes that trailed this other I'd become:
Gemini Girl,
wearing the same clothes for days

because that's what drifters do,
stay rugged and travel light.

Lean into a pillar
near the Hippodrome

and sniff where gladiators
once cracked their whips,

the gravel worn down by wheels
and centuries of teeth
into the park's fine dust.

Where the dogs just lie around now
and dream
without fences or chains.

Like pillows,
like sundials or compasses,

their sleeping paws stretched
in a direction
impossible to map,

where faces blur into one
and a name no longer matters.

I went behind the scenes . . . [and]
found there the violet coffin
~ *from a letter from George Bernard Shaw to Stella Campbell*

Actually, it was an old red shoebox
mined from the cave of a musty closet
and my son stood by as I lit a stub
of sage over the puffed pink breast
of a dead robin he'd found, supine
and stiff on the backyard brick. Had it fallen
from the purple crown of a nearby jacaranda?
Maybe it was that shadow of a hawk
I'd seen circling, eying nests clustered high
in the arms of the eucalyptus. The roaring,
feathery draft, honing in on heat and noise.
Some think it strange that Shaw watched
the remains of his mother being burned,
but if it were me, my bones, I wouldn't mind.
Others making a moment of it, the *materia*,
the fire of life forcing change. The way
mothering this boy has worn us both
to something precious that glints,
if a bit battered around the edges,
like a favored antique spoon reached for
from the drawer of all others. The door
of the furnace is beautiful. *It looked cool, clean,*
sunny, though no sun could get there. Nails and ashes
and samples of bone. My son wants to see
into it, the bird, its stopped clockwork,
the real thing. *People are afraid to see it;*
but it is wonderful. Shaw laughed and felt his mother
laughing right behind him, her feet to the flame,
bursting miraculously into ribbons of streaming,
smokeless scarlet. Sifting dust, the hours, my son and I
inspect death, *little tongs* in our hands, little handles
without misgiving. Scattering ourselves eagerly
across the garden, sudden wings and the shadow
of a bird passing over, sweeping us up
into its sieve as if to say: *O grave, where is thy victory?*

JUBILATE DEO

(A heroic tiara of sonnets through the persona of a time-traveling mother)

I postpone death by living, by suffering, by error,
by risking, by giving, by losing.
~ *Anaïs Nin, from* The Diary of Anaïs Nin 1931-1934

Butterflies

(the Archduke and the Cruiser)

And then *Lexias pardalis* tapped my wrist.
I was bent to the soil, to tender spires,
the sugar snaps my fingers worked to twist
about rough-hewn sticks, silken wire.
I watched his beauty unfold, the velvet black
wings beating time, his blunt blades' subtle force
against my skin: ephemeral, raw.
My thoughts floated to you, a naked pulse
our crossed paths struck, unveiled, briefly brushing.
Who knows why the heart takes flight, the forest inside
suddenly lit with bright knots fluttering?
This tinkered earth now swarms and swoons with life.
I plunge my hands and strum the pitch morass,
into it, too soon, I know my time must pass.

Behold the Beauty of the Lord

Into it, too soon, I know my time must pass . . .
Prayer my lips repeat at Sunday services,
Death's bee buzzing each ear of rose-stained glass,
each hallowed hollow, thrummed with hymnal music
that rocks the rigid pew, fueling desire.
The body is a tyrant, and I its cheerful
slave. In this public space I claim it: fire,
even my torn knee, where a hairpin, toppled
from my curls, pierced soft skin. You'd wrestled me
to the rug, spilled your confession from behind.
Memory soars now and I struggle to kneel.
Pain and ease, like water and mead, one finds,
are sometimes mixed. But this song's composed of love
and we drink with joy its ravishing cup.

Hummingbird

And we drink with joy its ravishing cup,
take to vein our ruddy syrups, sweet
as outside my window, nursing a glass teat,
this tiny, flitting sugar feeder sucks, needle
beak shot to the red smack faster
than stray lightning cracks a tree, faster still
than a ghost-girl walking smuggles her pills
and my mind grows wings and I remember
a brother resurrected as human harpsichord
but even before, long obsessions with
what it took to quell the paternal roar:
ampules, elixirs, the bottle's glowing hell
I poured unto each addled orifice,
Father, no more shall I hate you, anymore, myself.

The Children in Black

Father, no more shall I hate you, anymore, myself. Tell
me, what kind of mother says such things? In
the marketplace, they've fled. My darlings
scattered to steaming kiosks, tinseled pockets
and the dark deuce of their matching tunics
flown far from sight. Think of Rome. Paris.
Where would I be, if not here, haggling carrots?
Nowhere but the white-hot center of this
line, paying forward my precious time
for heartier futures, nourished soups.
Sometimes the moment opens like a fat
gold broth and strange scents suddenly wafted set
the wild clock ticking. And then I lose my cool
like a child who loves to break her own rules.

Jubilate Deo

Like a child who loves to break her own rules,
all the ponies bolting, her barn door razed.
The lyrics *Only women in cages*
can stand this kind of night graze blurry
pools from a buried past. Why not
imagine grace, getting a Holy Roller on
without an upper hand, say, palm to palm,
verse conjuring? This plush nave, my curved divan,
embraces me, stacked words tower and babble.
Here, the glimpsed ass of a room-cruising lover
is burning bush enough to fuel faith, still.
In death's dark veil, I will feel no ill.
Get up. Leave your cave. Go to him, Woman!
His flesh is multiplying like the stars of heaven.

She Lights the Sky at Dusk

His flesh is multiplying like the stars of heaven,
her hips cleaved open, the silt bed receives.
On crazed currents of the sea where I was born,
my shell rose, strung from silence, fathoms deep.
Swirl of copper, nickel, iron, cobalt,
and always the blood-jeweled teeth threatening
to clip my tale short, I swam toward light: surface.
I have no theory of radiance or kings,
Daughter, only remember always to make
a joyful sound. And loud. Your beauty's ring
surrounds this sinking sun; it is done. Take
these totems, your nautical wand. I'm falling
fast, lost to shadow, green sleep, the dreaming mist . . .
. . . and then *Lexias pardalis* tapped my wrist.

ESCAPE

I have burned like a lamp and have lit the world.
Now I am sooty from the smoke.
~ *Attar, from* The Conference of Birds

Ziggy

I don't know where I'm going from here but I promise it won't be boring. ~David Bowie

I thought of you today
from the corner of the classroom
near the terrarium tank
where a Chilean rose-haired tarantula hides
in her hollowed-out log.
My students were reading poems
and I was feeling a little sick
with a cough I can't quite shake.
I'd worn my T-shirt from London
that carries your face etched in shadow,
you who radiate life now
from the Valley of Death. Stretched
across my chest in gray poly-cotton blend,
your one weird eye resting
in the cusp between my cleavage,
touching my heart there,
I could rise above the aftertaste,
the orange medicinal syrup
that kept me dancing for the kids
whose hatched plots and wild songs
you would definitely dig.
Diamond Dog. Black Labrador
eating coal from the Grimmest tales
only to vomit back roses,
you've taught us to dwell in
the dimmest caves inside
and drift there alone, lushest stars
of our own unknowing. Queen Bitch,
oh you Spider from Mars
in your glitter boots and elevator legs,
silver twigs, two ghosts aflame
singing us to there and the cratered beyond.
What can you say to a svelte man-cat
decked out in rainbow suits
and rugged hairdos, studded chaps,
and violet Stratocasters, neon keyboards
on cosmic pedestals, supernatural
swagger of feminine divine,
the hero who launched our world?

They've found five asters
in the shape of a constellation
that resembles lightning,
a zagging bolt in the sky
swerving toward Virgo and Libra,
and named it after you, Ziggy,
and if we step outside
after midnight
when sleep makes ashes of our eyes
and the heavens gleam darkest,
astronomers say
for years to come—lucky us
—we might just see it.

The Fiery Stride

There's a girl in Nigeria
with five men an hour

Who make the decision for her

Whether or not
to lift her dress

Whether or not
to put child's play aside

But to breathe another day
means they'll come

When they want
so keep still and take it

It's what the Fathers demanded
blood for their blizzard

The sting that still won't silence
my sisters unprotected

She who watches
through the slit of a tent

As the sun burns holes
across a black savannah plain

Another night of raids
another body trying to erase

Some shine from her own
just like the other girl on her back

On an Alabama road
wishes he'd hurry up and finish

Her hand reaching
for the point of a star

Twinkling behind his head
like the spinning mobile

Above her crib she'd reach for
when her mama said *shush*

And wound the music key tighter

It's how you wonder what you are
and why wouldn't you instead

Reach for the undulating flank
of a drooling grunter

Trespassing on top of you
(the perfect grail of your cheek)

To find the handle, the trigger
the long cold barrel

Sprouting inside his back pocket
like stalks of hay

You'd chew
walking home from school

The dream of trains
and bus tickets

A classroom in some city
mixed palettes of humans

A mirror to strive toward
a landscape to stride through

Breathing the thought of that alone

Ticks the clock radically into
new zones of possibility

The sun's gold fingertip pointing
toward horizon's dark edge

As the cock crows
around the campfire or barn

Or wherever our girl lies
waiting for this man to finish

Coming like a bullet
to the base of his skull

As his throat explodes
his body lurches

And a shower of light falls
all around her

Bright-red water
like a diamond in the sky

Shattering
and she'll dive right in

Born again

Letting it cover her
up above the world so high

Red Hibiscus

~for Frances Farmer

Dear Woman Before Your Time,
dark barricade in an oversized coat,
a gorgeous storming of every set.

Art is not commerce, you snarled, wings
of your blond mane blown back,
the wildest rhythm on the range.

Scenes they forced you to play, lines
unfit for a dog: rotting garbage
hefted in a hot Hollywood gutter.

You wrote poetry too.
I'm not a glamour girl, you hissed,
siding with the Communists. Then, no chair,

water, or break for ten hours straight. Unkempt
orbits of contracts: black holes set in stone,
dictated by dicks that kept unzipping,

pounding the frames of starlets silly.
I wasn't made for this! Come and get me, you cried.
And Odets, that Golden Boy, arrived,

stuck his pen in your vitalist organs.
Even then you kept on ticking,
kicked that shit clean in.

Volcanoes for eyes, veins in flames
while mother waited in the wings.
Love that was not love, lacking identity itself.

I'm not you and I never will be, Mama!
But the self gone missing feeds
until its prey goes haywire.

And a cortex fried to the core
keeps fists and voices at bay,
your world splayed beautiful, crazy as a loon.

Tell me the alternative ending again?
The one about excised troupes, swift erasure
of a gender's worst predators?

Boots to the ground, the warrior marching
to a truer female tune?
You knew, Frances, singing beyond your time.

The stranger birthed inside sent forth,
more familiar than family.
Not the face imagined for you

that had nothing to do with.
Not the girl you never became
but narrowly missed.

That tragic other whose story
we've watched circle its tired loop too long.
Girl who self-edits in a hotel room,

her wrist a rush of color cut down:
red hibiscus in full bloom.
Not that one either.

But the one where art saves you.
Where the girl walks away and slays them
under a shower of bright and endless applause.

Body, heart, and mind kept solid,
her killer talent left intact, that is all.

Victorian Funeral Notice (Glass Coffin)

Even though it's a time of danger, maybe we are about to be free.
~ Gloria Steinem, at a preview of Annie Leibovitz's exhibition *WOMEN*: New Portraits, 2016

And now I see her in a box,
the girl I was back then.

I stand beside the glass cocoon
where the body's stretched out

inside, run my hands along
its cold crystal ceiling. Auroras

in the mind light up, color bleeds
across this sky's membered flesh.

There is no lid or seam to pry
my fingers through. The corpse

won't be tampered with. What's
done is, and where do you go

from here? Glance back. Snap
a pic like any good museum rat,

note the still life made
of her features, the constellating

gaze of dead lips and eyes. You've
dressed her in her best baptismal

whites, wads of lilies, pink-pearled
ribbons an orbit,

a horseshoe yoke
the winning beast and rider wear.

Blooms circle her skull, the
birthed sex of them

sewn to a crown embalmed
in time. Signaling the end

of a very long race, years
of struggle and what you

fought for erased. At what
you thought was the finish line.

The Red Opera

I kept running outside
to check how high
the spirea had grown,

dive-bombing my nose
into the asterisk clusters
that smelled faintly

of medicine and cake,
raspberry, conical
in breast-like mounds

the bees would not stop buzzing.

I kept wondering when
the next bomb would drop.

Should I keep running outside
to catch how fabulously

the fire and smoke
might volumize the horizon?

I kept wondering when someone
besides everyone I knew
could stop crying in the shadows.

Standing at the sink
in stunned silence,

listening to news
breaking over the suds and dishes.

We kept wiping our eyes
when the dinner guests weren't looking.

When would someone
make it stop,
this killing of beauty?

I had to keep reminding myself
we were riding this train together.

Where the flatcars
have no walls,

our bodies exposed
to the brutalist elements.

Skin peeled back,
naked, new creatures.

Our raw bones
and uncovered flesh,

the quick wind smarting
in blizzards and heat.

The dark made thicker,
our membranes thinner,
as we passed through tunnels,

layers of epidermis
sheer as shaved fennel.

It became impossible to pray.

But you couldn't help notice
the sprung doors
of the human aviary,

how with our cages left open,
a conference of hearts

fluttered in choirs
of flickering signals:

a red opera rising up.

People waved across the boulevard,
across stations
and airport waiting rooms,

spinning turnstiles
and Washington Square Park.

Even the Rose Bowl,
the county art museum,
and Smithsonian Center,

up to the Rocky Mountain Highs
you could hear it
and along the Sweet Plains of Georgia.

Down, down to the ocean boardwalks
and our bedrooms,

where all the windows and doors
were blast wide open,

filling the sky
with a plague of wings and songs.

The Fall

Sugar dissolves on a rim   not meant to be   breached   at least

in my mind   the crystals cling   despite my earnest   tilling

I am a traveler   wanting   to chain myself   to the strangest files

tinsel disruptions   all-in complicit   drawing   my hot and cold comforts

before final vote   hope the thing   didn't quite stick   its landing

centuries of feathers   in the spawning   and here we are   change

that would not be denied   the inevitable coming   even in   darkest times

our waves churn on   rising leaves   fling themselves   like Mardi Gras   girls

from vaults of trees   from gem-green balconies   clouds unlatching   skirts

of sheer and billowing   smoke   as baby slips her lips   from the nipple

Everything Crumbling Becoming Something New

When my baby told me   she wanted to be a boy   some part of me

had to die   slip away   like good mourners do   politely monk-like   the mother

of monasteries   drowning myself   my crushed head   a vat   of liquid

smoke   tasting of saffron   paint   letting it choke me   taking up the green

knife   the Spain in me   I was born to slice myself   into   little infinite

mirror stabs   cracked again   I'd have to   fall on it   muffle my cries

rushing wings   of birdsong memory   the hour's dusky passing   my girl

taking off   changing form   midflight   misty vestiges   shed   letting her go

so a son could enter   letting it go   just as we did   your every dress   cave of

my closet's harkening   skirts and gold-flecked minis   the black velvet strapless

poofs of yellow tulle   even the blue taffeta   from the chic boutique

in the Jewish Quarter   where the old Algerian   in fedora   and double-breasted

suit   directed us back   to the Seine   walking us halfway there   his simple

kindness   wanting to slap myself   my American offense   offering money

his eyes   crushed blossoms   where I come from   another shade of green

gets worshipped   more than being human   imagine selling your birthright

America   my mess of pottage   imagine giving birth   all over again

the two of you   going through it   again   child   woman   now man

all your multitudes   I'm learning to sing you   little green   little shorn-headed hero

your mother   an orphan   shrouds   for my gone girl   my vanity my mirage

a desert   of selves   boundless and bare   we bury ourselves   thinking greater than

a shattered visage   not you   your fledgling harmonies   bold your beauty   your many

within   sometimes sad   sometimes scary   refrains   thank you   thank you

for teaching me   to listen   sounds   who knew I   no   who knew you could make

As through Stony Ground the Green Shoots Break

and the spirit grinds its glass
to darker powders
the sun
a lazy Susan spinning light
behind trick clouds
yellow eye
bloated to red
in the year of our Unmaker
swollen
like a fish
in scarlet rapture
ruddy
as if rays had scorched him
from inside
a magnifying glass
held to the soul's distorted prism
We begot this
ochreous stain
rust
never sleeping
blood processes bearing
down for centuries
No worse than self-entombment
behind veneers
of pure
and polished deadwood
marble chrome disguises
I'd say
iron and decay
at least denote
vim and zing
a breath of life despoiling
celebrating water's natural masterpiece
I like to think of it
licking it
this way
the virtue of iron
being so fond
of getting itself rusted
crying over matter
shape and shadow

shifting as
the hours wear on
and imagination
disturbs us inside
our scrutiny of nothing
but this stain
this stain
we raise beyond the unmaking
color of blood
the river runs on
our salvation
a Loving cup
full of so many
hands now
lift

Glass-Bottom Boat

Because there's so much color to admire below
but feeling a little sick
on my bench with the swaying,
our stalled and stationary drift,
I had to look down through glass
with the other ogling families
in hoodies and parkas,
the better to see where shoals
of orange garibaldi swarmed
through streaming algae,
soft as in slow-motion dreaming.
You cannot fish particular species
protected by the state,
our captain said. And we nodded in silence.
It always heartens me to hear it:
For he will pluck my feet out of the net. . .
In the wide and delicate pond of humankind,
if only such care were taken with us all.

Escape (Fugue State #3)

I was wiping the sharpest corners of myself clean away,
all recognizable features, erasing a learned percentage
so the nothing me might emerge. I mean that
more than energetically, more than the kelvins necessary
to revive a childlike memory of riding seatbelt-less
in the back of a sky-blue station wagon, the Kodachrome sea
passing by in slideshow sections of the rear glass
or my glances forward at the flawed and beautiful faces
who'd made me. Innocent. It's all washed out
with the tide now. I'll let insects stake my elegies from here.
Even the silverfish showed up to wave their antennae,
scurrying out from under the cat's kibble dish. My naked heel
does nothing but plant itself on bathroom tile and watch,
like my eyes know Nirvana when they reel from it, random glimpses
that set the mind's basement ablaze. At this point in history,
anything could happen. As usual. Freedom snaps on camouflage,
playing hide-and-seek down dangerous corridors. Vintage street
fronts suddenly burst their pink bougainvillea brains
in my reveries alongside graves, crumbling hollows, and Roman-like
porticos, the faint aroma of zest drizzles from the scraped knees
of oranges. I'm awake and streaming coffee, strong and dark
as ten Arabian nights. If that's what's left, so be it. Something
fluent and otherworldly's afoot, menacing as dreams seized
and shaken into the organic matter of a letter-lined valise.
We've called a new guard in as bodies of wanderers toss
their last sheets to the bitterest on-screen winds. Monuments fall,
the people weep. So long, stones. Hello, fuzzy cities. I'll
know I've arrived when sirens serenade me to sleep.

Odyssey

Into the folds
of endless appetites
I've tucked
some yellow cheese, raw
barley & green honey, two kinds
of acorns & the fruit
of the cornel tree, *dark*
at its root
with a flower-like milk.
This black ship,
fluid in wind, baggy
& blown about
its midlife seas. Love,
that faithful canine at the gate
dropping its ears
as time, the only master, passes.
Twenty-five years, Argos.
I've come this far
to find you
and as with all beloved things,
knife my eyes open wide
and watch you shatter, tissue clouds
& funeral cake
crashing down, sugar
& tears, my shrouds for dead soil.
The place I put my mouth to next
and dig, ravenous.
The only way to forget.
To grow the past
a new head of joy. Lord knows
I've stuck mine so far into muck, I barely
breathe anymore.
The only way I've learned
to lick bitter waters
riding a violent sea home.
This map
made of gold, pinned
close to me and bloody
with monsters.
I call it my life.

Requiem

Go love without the help of any thing on earth.
~ William Blake, from "The angel that presided o'er my birth"

Go with stones in your pocket,
the leaden call of clear water.
This wild stream
you're running after,
a plunging dream
and wrecking ball, sunk.
From ice, songs rise, liquid
tracking each muscular rose,
each bone unearthed,
wrung from the dead. Isn't it nice
to think tomorrow is a new day
with no mistakes yet? The stains
on your skin, really wounds
rubbed clean, rolled in clover.
So much spit and polish,
this life, a lantern, saints
smiling in the dark,
your crown of skulls releasing
a vast and solitary light.

Acknowledgements

The American Journal of Poetry: "Drought," "The Fiery Stride,"
   "What the Rain Made"
American Literary Review: "An Hour North of Lee Vining, California"
Askew: "sometimes i want to look away"
Atticus Review: "Little Red Car," "Odyssey," "Victorian Funeral Notice,"
   "When the Work Runs Out Again"
Catamaran: "Everything Crumbling Becoming Something New,"
   "I went behind the scenes . . . [and] found there the violet coffin"
Connotation Press: "Portrait of Cafe with Young Schizophrenic Couple,"
   "Recipe for Disaster," "The Red Opera"
Diode: "As through Stony Ground the Green Grass Breaks,"
   "Autumn Deluge," "Escape: Fugue State #3," "Touched"
Fjords Review: "Back Then I Wanted to Paint like Rauschenberg,"
   "Butterflies," "Jubilate Deo"
Green Mountains Review: "December 20, 2016"
The Los Angeles Review: "Bricolage"
Love's Executive Order: "On O'Hara's Birthday"
Narrative Magazine: "Requiem"
The New York Times: "November"
Nimrod International Journal of Prose and Poetry: "Artisanal Baptismal,"
   "Home," "Stripped, Genesis"
Plume: "Burnt Offerings," "Pompeii"
Poetry Bay: "She Lights the Sky at Dusk"
Public Pool: "Red Hibiscus"
Raleigh Review: "Glass-Bottom Boat"
South Florida Poetry Journal: "Broken Kingdom," "Twenty Years Later
   in a Kitchen"
Tabula Poetica: "City of Angels"
Thrush: "Fugue State #2"
Tupelo Quarterly: "Glimmers and Limbo (Fugue State #1)"
Verdad Magazine: "After"
Vinyl Poetry: "Ziggy"

"Everything Crumbling Becoming Something New"
   won the 2018 Fischer Prize
"An Hour North of Lee Vining, California" was a finalist for the 2016
   American Literary Review Award in Poetry
"Artisanal Baptismal," "Home," and "Stripped, Genesis" were finalists
   for the 2016 Pablo Neruda Prize for Poetry
"Glimmers and Limbo (Fugue State #1)" was a finalist for
   Tupelo Quarterly's TQ11 Call and Response
   Poetry Contest

"Fugue State #2" was nominated for 2017 Best of the Net by
        Thrush Poetry Journal
"Ziggy" is for Rainn Wilson
"On O'Hara's Birthday" is for Matthew Dickman
"An Hour North of Lee Vining, California" is for Joseph Millar
"Red Hibiscus" is for Gigi Bermingham
"Victorian Funeral Notice (Glass Coffin)" is for Holiday Reinhorn
"The Red Opera" is for Christopher O'Riley

"Book epigraphs" are from Wolfram von Eschenbach's *Parzival* and
        Talking Heads' "This Must Be the Place (Naive Melody)"
"On O'Hara's Birthday" includes a lyric from Laurie Anderson's
        "Sharkey's Day"
"After" references Wallace Stevens's "The Plain Sense of Things"
"Twenty Years Later in a Kitchen" is a Golden Shovel inspired
        by Gwendolyn Brooks's "kitchenette building"
"Glimmers and Limbo (Fugue State #1)" uses found phrases from Gaston
        Bachelard's *The Poetics of Reverie* and a line from Indigo Minute
"Touched" includes a quote from Edna St. Vincent Millay's "Renascence"
"City of Angels" includes a quote from David Bowie's "Soul Love"
Nods to Robert Olen Butler for inspiration on the heroic tiara of sonnets
"Jubilate Deo" references a line from Steely Dan's "Razor Boy"
Attar epigraph is from Sholeh Wolpé's translation of
        The Conference of the Birds
"Ziggy" epigraph is a quote from David Bowie's fiftieth-birthday concert
        at Madison Square Garden
"Red Hibiscus" was inspired in part by the movie *Come and Get It* and by
        the exhibit Cindy Sherman: *Imitation of Life*
        at the Broad Museum, 2016
"Glass-Bottom Boat" contains a phrase from Psalms 25:15
"Odyssey" was inspired by Emily Wilson's stunning translation of
        The Odyssey

This book is the winner of the 2018 Catamaran Poetry Prize for West Coast poets, generously underwritten by the RiskPress Foundation in Sebastopol, California. The Catamaran Poetry Prize is open to all West Coast poets living in the states of California, Alaska, Hawaii, Oregon, and Washington. The prize is open to submissions from November to March.

Please visit catamaranliteraryreader.com contact/submit or write to editor@catamaranliteraryreader.com for more information.

Many thanks to my friends and family for their love and support with my work here on earth. Special thanks to Liz, Rebecca, Nina, Holiday, Alex, Alexis, Fancher, Martin, James, Lans, Franz, Richard, Joe, Dorianne, Phil Abrams (my beloved who makes it all fly), Leslie, Laura Grillo, Gail Wronsky, John Gosslee, Andrew Sullivan, Catherine Segurson, Zack Rogow, Mona Moraru, Charlie Pendergast, and everyone at Catamaran. Robin Cass and everyone at Pacifica Graduate Institute, Mythological Studies Program.

This book is for my parents.

This book is set in 10 point Palatino Linotype
Designed by Charlie Pendergast and Kevin Connor
Printed in China
by Global PSD